SNAKES

By S.L. Hamilton

VISIT US AT
WWW.ABDOPUBLISHING.COM

Published by ABDO Publishing Company, 8000 West 78th Street, Suite 310, Edina, MN 55439. Copyright ©2010 by Abdo Consulting Group, Inc. International copyrights reserved in all countries. No part of this book may be reproduced in any form without written permission from the publisher. A&D Xtreme™ is a trademark and logo of ABDO Publishing Company.

Printed in the United States of America, North Mankato, Minnesota.
102009
012010

PRINTED ON RECYCLED PAPER

Editor: John Hamilton
Graphic Design: Sue Hamilton
Cover Design: John Hamilton
Cover Photo: Getty Images
Interior Photos: AP-pgs 8, 9, 28, & 29; Corbis-pgs 10, 11, 12, & 13; Getty Images-pgs 4, 5, 6, 7, 24, & 25; Jupiterimages-pgs 2 & 3; National Geographic-pgs 1, 19, 30 & 31; Peter Arnold-pgs 18, & 19; Photo Researchers-pgs 14, 15, 16, 17, 20, 21, 22, 23, 26, & 27; and Visuals Unlimited-pgs 14 & 32.

Library of Congress Cataloging-in-Publication Data

Hamilton, Sue L., 1959-
 Snakes / S.L. Hamilton.
   p. cm. -- (Xtreme predators)
 Includes index.
 ISBN 978-1-60453-994-3
 1. Snakes--Juvenile literature. 1. Title.
 QL666.Q6H334 2010
 597.96--dc22

                              2009045273

CONTENTS

XTREME

SNAKES

Nature has made snakes deadly and precise predators. Their speed, senses, and killing tools allow them to control the populations of small mammals, lizards, birds, fish and insects.

Xtreme Fact

Rattlesnake venom stuns prey immediately, and can kill small animals within 20 seconds.

VENOMOUS

SNAKES

Snake venom is a toxic saliva. The moment venom enters the body, it starts to destroy cells and begins to digest the prey even before it's dead.

Fierce Snake

Australia's fierce snake, also called an Inland Taipan snake, has the most toxic venom of any snake. Its poison is 50 times stronger than that of an Indian cobra. Despite of its name, the fierce snake is usually very calm and shy. No humans have been killed by this venomous, but easy-going reptile.

Xtreme Fact

A single bite from a fierce snake has enough poison to kill 100 human adults or 250,000 mice.

Most sea snakes are calm and shy. Few people have ever been envenomated.

Sea Snakes

Sea snakes live in the warm waters of the Indian and Pacific Oceans. Their venom is more poisonous than many land snakes, so their prey of fish and birds can't swim or fly away before the venom takes effect. The fast-acting poison quickly stops the prey's breathing and muscles. Luckily, sea snakes don't usually attack humans.

King Cobras

At 18 feet (5.5 m) in length, a king cobra is able to lift one-third of its body off the ground and look a person in the eye. It is even able to chase prey in this upright position. The venom from a king cobra causes severe pain and paralysis. In a few minutes, a bite victim's heart and lungs will stop working.

Xtreme Fact King cobra venom can kill a human in 15 minutes and an elephant within 3 hours.

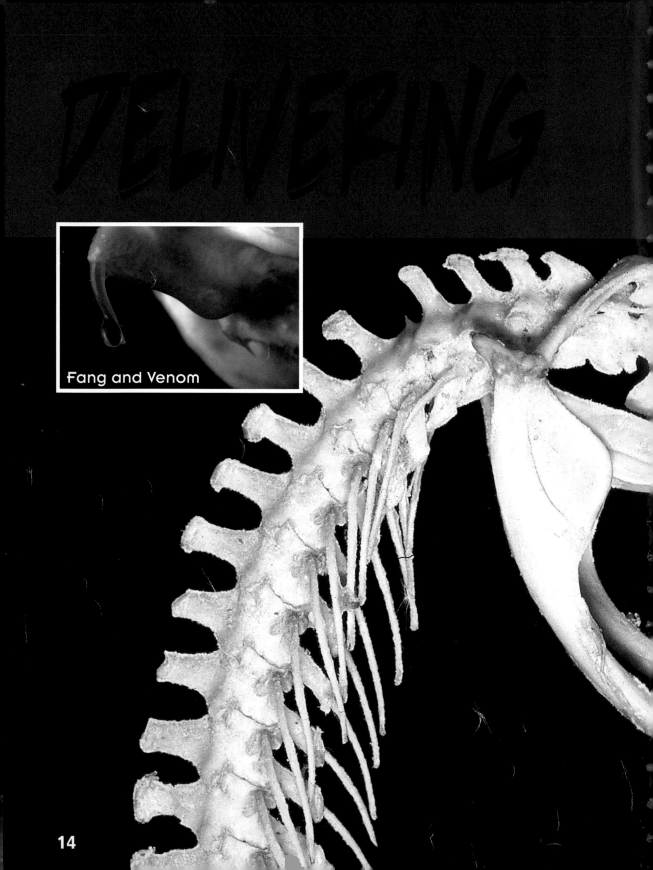

DELIVERING

Fang and Venom

VENOM

Most venomous snakes deliver their poison through fangs that work like hypodermic needles. The poison-filled saliva flows from small sacs in the snake's head and is shot through the snake's long, hollow teeth directly into their victim's flesh.

Spitting

Spitting cobras are able to deliver their venom by spitting the poison at the eyes of their victims. Strong muscle contractions force the poison from the venom gland, blasting it out of their fangs. The cobra expels a gust of air from its lungs at the same time, spraying the venom out like liquid from an aerosol can.

Xtreme Fact

Spitting cobras can shoot their venom a distance of 6.5 feet (2 m).

SNAKE

Pit Organ

SENSES

Snakes have special senses to help them find prey. The forked tongue picks up chemical molecules on the ground and

Heat-sensitive pit organs let some snakes detect prey by their warmth.

in the air. In the roof of a snake's mouth is the Jacobson's organ. It processes the chemical odors and sends the information to the snake's brain. Some snakes, such as pit vipers, have pit organs on either side of their face that act as heat sensors. These organs allow the snake to "see" warm-blooded animals from the heat of their bodies.

CONSTRICTING

Snakes do not chew their food, they swallow it whole.

SNAKES

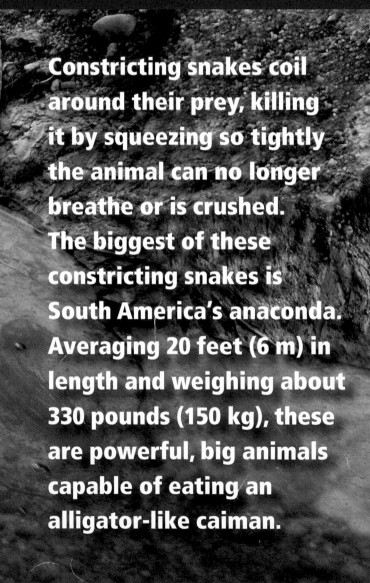

Constricting snakes coil around their prey, killing it by squeezing so tightly the animal can no longer breathe or is crushed. The biggest of these constricting snakes is South America's anaconda. Averaging 20 feet (6 m) in length and weighing about 330 pounds (150 kg), these are powerful, big animals capable of eating an alligator-like caiman.

Pythons

Pythons, the longest constricting snake, are tree-climbers. They eat birds, as well as small mammals, monkeys, and pigs. The Asiatic reticulated python is the world's longest snake, reaching 33 feet (10 m) in length. Pythons ambush their prey, waiting until their victim is nearby and then coiling around it and squeezing their meal to death.

Xtreme Fact

Some people keep boa constrictors to hunt mice and rats in their yards.

Boa Constrictor

Central and South American boa constrictors hunt at night using heat-sensitive scales on their bodies. Boas eat small mammals, as well as bats and birds. To capture flying prey, boas hang from tree branches or cave openings, and grab their meal from the air, constricting around them.

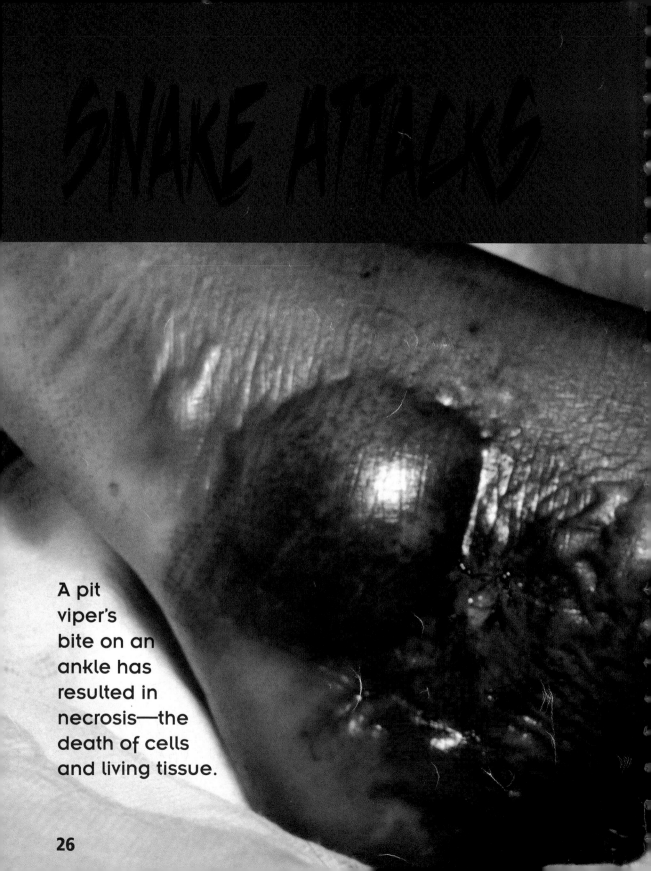

SNAKE ATTACKS

A pit viper's bite on an ankle has resulted in necrosis—the death of cells and living tissue.

ON HUMANS

About 5 million snakebites occur worldwide every year, including 125,000 deaths. People who quickly receive antivenin treatments usually survive these bites.

Venom is milked from a pit viper to make antivenin.

Xtreme Quote
"Look before you leap, for snakes among sweet flowers do creep."

HUMAN ATTACKS

Heavy snake hunting, such as annual rattlesnake roundups, greatly reduce snake populations, often causing increased rodent populations and other ecological unbalances.

ON SNAKES

THE

Aerosol
A liquid enclosed under pressure and then released as a fine spray.

Antivenin
Also called antivenom. A liquid used to treat and stop the effects of a bite from venomous creatures, such as snakes. Antivenin is created by injecting an animal or eggs with a small amount of a specific snake's venom. The host animal produces antibodies against the venom, which can then be taken from its blood and used to treat humans.

Envenomate
To inject poison, such as venom, by biting or stinging. A venomous snake may bite a person without releasing its venom. Only when a snake injects poison is it said to envenomate a person.

GLOSSARY

Hypodermic Needle
A hollow needle used to inject fluid under the skin.

Jacobson's Organ
A sensory organ that snakes use to smell their prey.

Paralysis
Unable to move.

Saliva
A watery liquid found in the mouth. The liquid helps with chewing and swallowing food.

Toxic
Poisonous and sometimes deadly. Snake venom is toxic.

Venom
A poisonous liquid that some reptiles such as snakes, Gila monsters, and scorpions use for killing prey, and for defense.

INDEX